W9-CKZ-115

A GIFT FOR:

FROM:

DATE:

A Baby Changes Everything

Thomas Nelson, Inc. titles may be purchased in bulk for educational, business, fund-raising, or sales promotional use. For information, please e-mail SpecialMarkets@ThomasNelson.com.

Unless otherwise noted, all Scripture references are from New King James Version ©1979, 1980, 1982, 1992, Thomas Nelson, Inc.

Designed by Susan Browne Design, Nashville, TN

Images: cover (and others): pregnant belly © Takako Chiba/NEOVISION/Getty Images. manger detail © R. Gino Santa Maria, 2007. Used under license from Shutterstock.com. toddler hand © Andrejs Pidjass, 2007. Used under license from Shutterstock.com. abstract bg behind hand © Aij Abele, 2007. Used under license from Shutterstock.com. bright star © Dan Collier, 2007. Used under license from Shutterstock.com. canvas textu © graemo, 2007. Used under license from Shutterstock.com. detail of square pattern texture paper © replickater, 2007. Used under license from Shutterstock.com. floral vector © Sanjar, 2007. Used under license from Shutterstock.com. / 1: gift tag © magicinfoto, 2007. Used under license from Shutterstock.com. swirls vector (pg 1 and others) © Dmitry Remesov, 2007. Used under license from Shutterstock.com. / 3: (and others): bright star © Dan Collier, 2007. Used under license from Shutterstock.com. / 4: dove © Corbis/Veer. snowflakes © Photodisc / 10-11: girl © Dynamic Graphics. / 13: rollercoaster image © Corbis/Veer. / 15: (and others) floral vector © Sanjar, 2007. Used under license from Shutterstock.co / 17: Angel before sunset © LeroySmart, 2007. Used under license from Shutterstock.com. / 18: vector floral swirls and flowers © Merve Poray, 2007. Used under license from Shutterstock.com. / 19: baby eyes © Roman Barelko, 2007. Used under license from Shutterstock.com. / 20-21: baby foot in hand © Digital Vision. / 24: Green traffic light © Tihis, 2007. Used under license from Shutterstock.com. / 26: broken Christmas ball © eAlisa, 2007. Used under license from Shutterstock.com. / 29: snow globe © David Fischer/Getty Images. / 30: Baby hand © Dimitri, 2007. Used under license from Shutterstock.com. / 32-33: Vector swirls © hcss5, 2007. Used under license from Shutterstock.com. / 35: motel sign © Karin Lau, 2007. Used under license from Shutterstock.com. / 37: calendar © Photodisc. / 38: gold star ornament © Veer. / 40-41: snowscape © Digit Vision. / 42-43: new born fingers © Curtis Kautzer, 2007. Used under license from Shutterstock.com. / 44-45: Mother and baby © Dimitri, 2007. Used under license from Shutterstock.com. / 48: star tree topper © Stephen Coburn, 2007. Used under license from Shutterstock.com. / 49 (and others): Pleiades (M45) starry sky © CyMaN, 2007. Used under license from Shutterstock.com. / 50: angel statue © Lori Martin, 2007. Used und license from Shutterstock.com. / 57: bread and wine © Magdalena Kucova, 2007. Used under license from Shutterstock.com. / 58-59: baby feet in father hand © Chepko Danil Vitalevich, 2007. Used under license from Shutterstock.com. / 60-61: dove © Balakirev Vladimir, 2007. Used unde license from Shutterstock.com. round frame vector © Dmitry Remesov, 2007. Used under license from Shutterstock.com.

Project Manager: Lisa Stilwell

ISBN-10: 1-4041-8734-0

ISBN-13: 978-1-4041-8734-4

Printed and bound in the United States

www.thomasnelson.com

08 09 10 11 12—6 5 4 3 2 1

FOREWORD BY
FAITH HILL

a baby
CHANGES
everything

Rev. KK Wiseman

Craig Wiseman

Tim Nichols

THOMAS NELSON
Since 1798

NASHVILLE DALLAS MEXICO CITY RIO DE JANEIRO BEIJING

FOREWORD

I first heard this song about four years ago and I immediately fell in love with it. I was genuinely moved. Craig, KK, and Tim have found a way to take the oldest of stories, the birth of baby Jesus, and make it relevant to us today, with the hope and optimism that defines Christmas. I am so thankful and fortunate to have been given the opportunity to record the song for my Christmas album, because a baby did, and does, really change everything.

—*Faith Hill*

Teenage girl
much too young
Unprepared for
what's to come
A baby changes everything

Not a ring on her hand
All her dreams and
all her plans
A baby changes everything
A baby changes
everything

a gift

This Christmas gift is for you.

It may not be quite what you were anticipating.

It may be unexpected.

Or you may think it's **too much and all wrong for you.**

But it's just right,

It's a gift more precious than silver or gold.

And it's perfect for you.

This is *the* Christmas gift,
The *only* gift, really . . .

A BABY

It's for *you*. It's for everyone.
Everywhere.

Will you accept it?

why you?

You have found favor with God… —Luke 1:30

Why not you?

You are beautiful . . .

special . . .

wonderful . . .

Yes, YOU.

prepare

Ready for a miracle?

Nobody's ever *really* ready for a **miracle**.

Ready for a baby?

Ready or not, it's coming sure as Christmas.

Just like the first big drop at the start of a rollercoaster —you absolutely know it's coming, it's what you signed on for, you're locked in, you've counted the clicks as the cars cranked higher and higher. You know what's coming, sort of. You know what's coming, and you're excited and terrified and you're short of breath and you feel ready to scream and you can't wait and you hope it never comes and you hope it comes soon and you…and…and…and…wheeeeeeee!

Yeah, you're never quite ready and you can hardly wait.

Terrifying. Terrific.

The man she loves
she never touched
How will she keep
his trust?
A baby changes
everything
A baby changes everything

And she cries...

Be not afraid. You are

never

CHRISTMAS AND THE *gift* OF CHRISTMAS IS YOUR REMINDER THAT YOU ARE NOT ALONE... YOU ARE NEVER ALONE.

alone

You have angels.

A BABY CHANGES EVERYTHING.

Rejoice…the Lord is with you…
— Luke 1:28

look

See the world with new eyes.

It's hard to judge others when you are

preoccupied with love.

A baby changes everything.

dreams

A DREAM IS WHAT MIGHT BE.

Even if they've faded, this Gift of Christmas will breathe new life into them.

To have a baby is to dream new dreams,
to dream further into the future than you ever have before.
This child will change who you are and who you will become.
From the first cry, your dreams will never be the same.

A baby is a dream come true.

She has to leave, go far away

Heaven knows she can't stay

A baby changes everything

go

A BABY GIVES YOU
COURAGE.

You'll do things for a baby
you'd never dream of doing
for **anyone** else.

For a child, you'll make a fool of yourself,
you'll give more than you thought you had.

For a child you'll be
**bigger, bolder,
braver, better.**

A baby changes everything.

lighten up

Nobody's perfect

when they have a baby.

A baby turns every parent into an improv artist doing the best they can with what they've got. Luckily, babies don't know if you're "doing it right."

Babies just know if you love them.

Forget the mistakes. Try again.

Life's like that, too.

Tears dry. Hurts heal.

We live and learn . . .

A baby changes everything.

plans

A baby is upsetting.
What doesn't it upset?

SCHEDULES,
STOMACHS,
HOUSEHOLDS,
  THE BEST LAID PLANS...
LIFE.

But for crying out loud, *it's a baby!*
Who cares!

First you're terrified
out of your mind.

Then you're thrilled.
And then it starts to sink in.

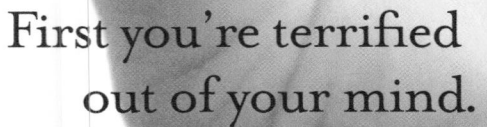

now?

You wonder how you got here . . . and where you'll go from here.

You think you can handle it. A baby is so small, after all.

There's nothing to be afraid of. Is there?
All the changes will be okay, right?
Nothing too drastic, right?

Nothing too fast, nothing too scary, nothing too . . . wheeeeee!

A baby changes everything.

She can tell

it's coming soon

But there's no place,

there's no room

A baby

changes everything

A baby changes everything

And she cries...

it's time

Find room.
Make room.

In your home. In your heart.

A baby is coming…

and that changes everything.

There was no room for them in the inn. —Luke 2:7

soon

No matter how ready
(or not)
you *think* you are, *nobody is.*

Everyone thinks they know
what will change when the
baby comes. Nobody does.

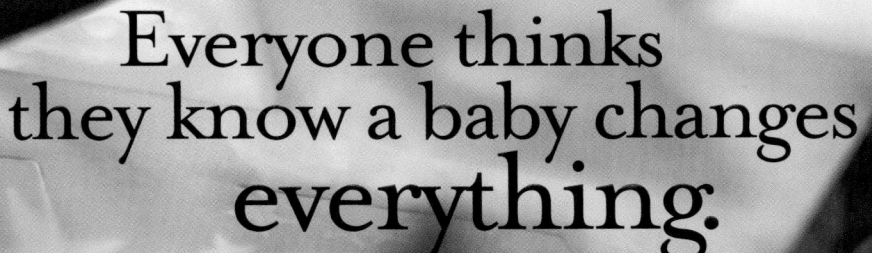

Everyone thinks
they know a baby changes
everything.

But they don't...
until it does.

Joy to the World!

A baby changes

joy

Behold, I bring you good tidings of great joy…
—Luke 2:14

A baby changes

And on earth peace, goodwill toward men!
—Luke 2:14

A baby changes

hope

*The light
shines in
the darkness…*
—John 1:5

A baby changes *love*

For God so loved the world…
—John 3:16

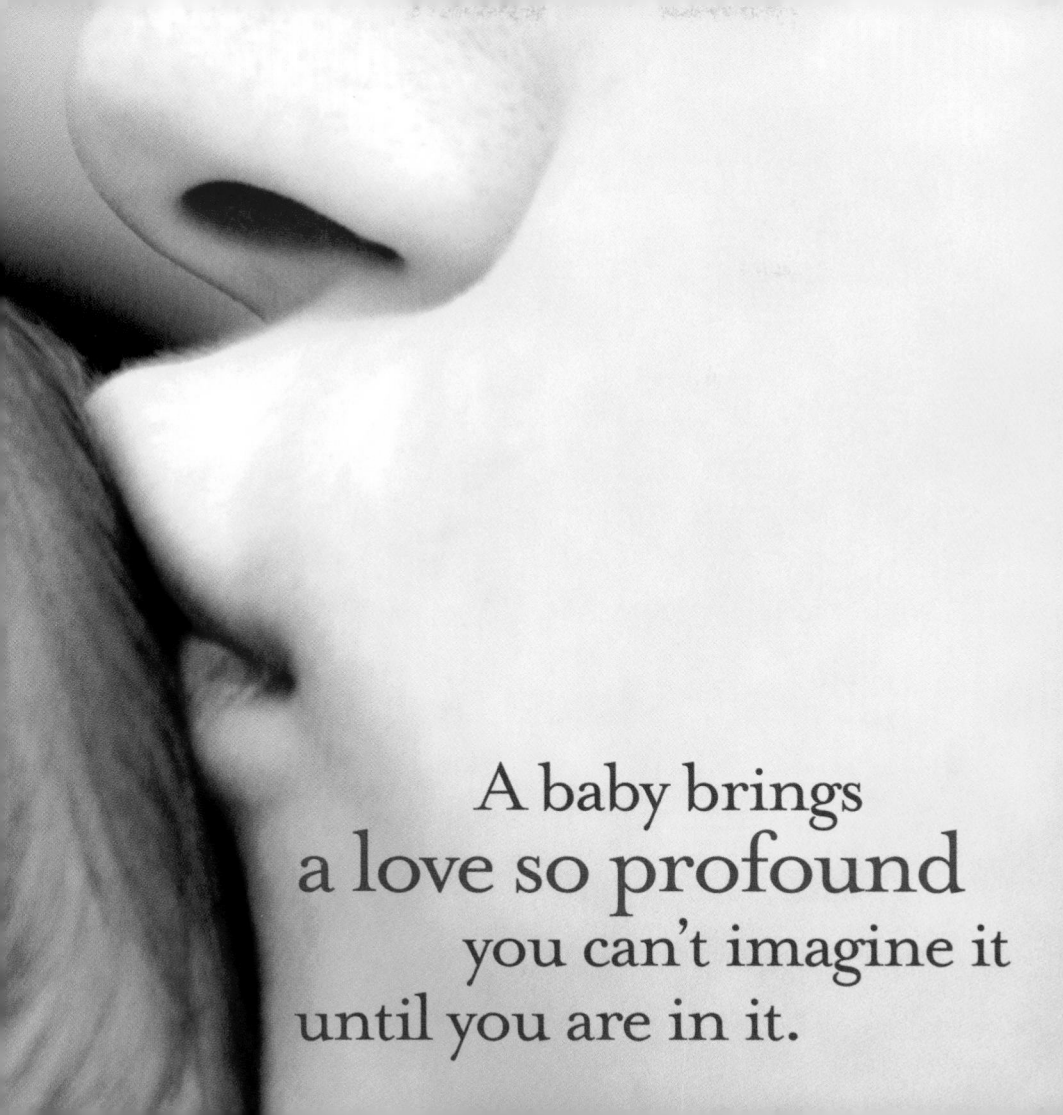

A baby brings
a love so profound
you can't imagine it
until you are in it.

Shepherds all gathered 'round

Up above a star shines down

A baby changes everything

A choir of angels sing
Glory to the newborn king
A baby changes everything

everything

everything

everything

The star . . .
went before them.
—Matthew 2:9

star

Starlight.

The sign.

This baby is special.

This is your baby.

What is the light that lights up your life?

What *light* do you follow?
What *light* do you seek?

What light seeks you?
A baby changes everything.

You can't have a baby alone.

No matter what your situation.
If you have a baby, you are going to need help…

Fortunately,
God has a way of sending
just the right help
at just the right moment.

A baby comes with angels.

A baby changes everything.

Behold. A baby. Your baby. *The* Baby.

Redemption…fresh start…new hope…

Go on, let it all out...let it all in.
It's Christmas.

And a baby changes everything.

*She brought forth
her firstborn Son,
and wrapped Him
in swaddling cloths,
and laid Him
in a manger...*
—Luke 2:7

My whole life was
turned around
I was lost
but now I'm found
A baby changes
everything

A baby changes *everything*

A wonder to hold.
A wonder to behold.

grace

Amazing
is the grace
that comes to find you
as gently as a newborn babe.

how sweet the sound…I once was lost…but now I'm found…

The Story Behind

A Baby Changes Everything

Ultimately, this song began with one tiny baby more than two thousand years ago. And a lot of fantastic things have happened as a result. No surprise though—a baby does change everything.

The journey began with KK writing a sermon which led to Craig and Tim writing a song, which then led to all three of us writing this book.

Not long after we wrote the song, we got the news that Faith Hill wanted to record it for her album *Fireflies*. Needless to say, we were thrilled, and we couldn't wait to hear her sing it. However, the long wait for this "baby" to be born had only just begun.

First, Faith told us she loved the song so much she didn't want it to get lost on an album. Instead, she wanted to wait and put it on her very first Christmas album. Of course we said we would wait—we had faith...and Faith...and faith in Faith. But then *Fireflies* did really well and the record label pushed back the Christmas album a year. And then her tour went really well, and the album got pushed back another year.

But finally, it happened. Faith went into the studio and out came a miracle. The wait was worth it—more than worth it.

We hope the song brings you "glad tidings of great joy." It is a special song to us. Craig and Tim are thrilled to get the opportunity to follow up their Grammy-winning Tim McGraw hit, "Live Like You Were Dying" with a Faith Hill song that also celebrates life (the two songs make a nice set). And for KK and Craig, this is their first writing collaboration in fifteen years of marriage (…changes everything).

The song itself is special, but the rest of the story is extraordinary. Many great writers have told it before—Matthew, Mark, and Luke are some of our favorites. Check 'em out!

Merry Christmas,

Craig, KK & Tim

Faith Hill

Since her debut single, "Wild One," held the number-one spot on Billboard's country singles chart for four weeks in 1994, Faith Hill has gone on to win five Grammys, four American Music Awards, three CMAs, and twelve Academy of Country Music awards. With hits like "The Way You Love Me," "Breathe," "This Kiss," and "Cry," Faith has become one of the most successful and recognizable stars in country music. She is married to fellow country superstar Tim

McGraw; the couple have three daughters. This year, Faith releases a much anticipated Christmas album, Joy to the World, featuring "A Baby Changes Everything" written by Tim Nichols, Craig Wiseman, and KK Wiseman.